The Belligerent Book of Movie Quotes

Danny Marianino

www.dannymarianino.com

DEDICATION

This book goes out to the movie fans that can watch a film and remember the horrible things said, in humor or in a threatening manner, and repeat them word for word in their everyday lives.

Acknowledgments

Layout by Danny Marianino
Cover Layout by Jay Fotos
Original Text Edited by Dolly Renea

Special Thanks: Tal and Rue Morgue Magazine, Mania .Com, LeglessCorpse.Com, Bullet Proof Action .Com, The Film Bar, Josh and Hell City Tattoo Festival, Heavy Metal Television, The Phoenix Film Foundation, Jay Fotos, Brandon Kinchen, The Midnite Movie Mamacita, Dan Stone, Kamal Ahmed, Dolly Renea, Tom Reardon and my amazing wife Krista Marianino.

You're a fucking ugly bitch. I want to stab you to death, and then play around with your blood. – Patrick Bateman in American Psycho (2000)

There is nothing inspirational in what you are about to read. This book is truly just a massive collection of distasteful and angry movie quotes. Most of this book carries foul language and is remarkably offensive.

In other words, you will find this quite entertaining.

Enjoy -

Danny Marianino

Well it appears to me that there can't be too many guys driving around this valley with an ape. – Cholla in Every Which Way But Loose (1978)

Even if I were blind, desperate, starved and begging for it on a desert island, you'd be the last thing I'd ever fuck. - Elvira Hancock in Scarface (1983)

When I watch you eat. When I see you asleep...When I look at you lately, I just want to smash your face in. – Barbara Rose in War of the Roses (1989)

What are you looking at butthead? – Biff Tannen in Back to the Future (1985)

You're a funny guy Sully, I like you. That's why I'm going to kill you last. – Matrix in Commando (1985)

Just remember what ol' Jack Burton does when the earth quakes, and the poison arrows fall from the sky, and the pillars of Heaven shake. Yeah, Jack Burton just looks that big ol' storm right square in the eye and he says, "Give me your best shot, pal. I can take it." – Jack Burton in Big Trouble in Little China (1986)

You are physically repulsive, intellectually retarded, you're morally reprehensible, vulgar, insensitive, selfish, stupid, you have no taste, a lousy sense of humor and you smell. You're not even interesting enough to make me sick. - Alexandra Medford in The Witches of Eastwick (1987)

You are nothing! If you were in my toilet I wouldn't bother flushing it. My bathmat means more to me than you! - Buddy in Swimming with Sharks (1994)

The Dude Abides - The Big Lebowski (1998)

I don't like your jerk-off name. I don't like your jerk-off face. I don't like your jerk-off behavior, and I don't like you, jerk-off. Do I make myself clear? - Malibu Police Chief in The Big Lebowski (1998)

Does Barry Manilow know that you raid his wardrobe? - John Bender in The Breakfast Club (1985)

You clinking, clanking, clattering collection of caliginous junk! – The Wizard in The Wizard of Oz (1939)

You're an emotional fucking cripple. Your soul is dog shit. Every single fucking thing about you is ugly. – Marcus in Bad Santa (2003)

Dead or alive, you're coming with me! - Murphy in RoboCop (1987)

Maybe I don't give a shit. Maybe I don't remember the last time I blew my nose either. Who the fuck are you, I should remember you? What, you think you like me? You ain't like me motherfucker. You a punk. I've been with made people, connected people. Who you been with? Chain-snatching, jive-ass, maricon motherfuckers. Why don't you get lost? Go ahead, snatch a purse. Come on, take a fucking walk. – Carlito Brigante in Carlito's Way (1993)

Your mama used to steal chickens out of the backyard until I blew her head off with a shotgun. – Mick in Teen Wolf (1985)

It was nothing like that penis breathe! - Elliot in E.T. the Extra-Terrestrial (1982)

I was in this bureau, when you were still popping zits on your funny face and jacking off to the lingerie section of the Sears catalog. – Pappas in Point Break (1991)

Well, you're mothers so poor I saw her kicking cans down the street and I said what you doing, she said, "Moving." - Junior in White Men Can't Jump (1992)

Owen loves his Momma in Throw Momma from the Train (1987)

You're gonna be nothing. You'll never get to first base. All you do is type, type, type, type, type, type. You sit there typing all day like a fat little pigeon.– Mrs. Lift in Throw Momma from the Train (1987)

Take this quarter, go downtown, and have a rat gnaw that thing off your face! – Buck Russell in Uncle Buck (1989)

The only reason you're living here is because me and my dad decided that your mom was really hot, and maybe we should just both bang her, and we'll put up with the retard in the meantime. - Dale Doback in Step Brothers (2008)

I'm mean, nasty and tired. I eat concertina wire and piss napalm, and I can put a round through a flea's ass at 200 meters. So why don't you go hump somebody else's leg, mutt face, before I push yours in. – Highway in Heartbreak Ridge (1986)

There's no way, no way, that you came from my loins. Soon as I get home, first thing I'm gonna do is punch your mamma in the mouth! - Buford T. Justice in Smokey and the Bandit (1977)

I despise rapists. For me, you're somewhere between a cockroach and that white stuff that accumulates at the corner of your mouth when you're really thirsty. But, in your case, I'll make an exception. - Cyrus Grissom in Con Air (1997)

You talkin' to me? You talkin' to me? You talkin' to me? Then who the hell else are you talking... you talking to me? Well I'm the only one here. Who the fuck do you think you're talking to? Oh yeah? OK. – Travis Bickle in Taxi Driver (1976)

You don't seem to want to accept the fact you're dealing with an expert in guerrilla warfare, with a man who's the best, with guns, with knives, with his bare hands. A man who's been trained to ignore pain, ignore weather, to live off the land, to eat things that would make a billy goat puke. In Vietnam his job was to dispose of enemy personnel. To kill! Period! Win by attrition. Well Rambo was the best. – Trautman in First Blood (1982)

Here's the thing...I don't give a tuppenny fuck about your moral conundrum, you meat-headed shit sack. - Bill 'The Butcher' Cutting in Gangs of New York (2002)

El Guapo only kills men. The Three Amigos (1996)

You dirt-eating piece of slime! You scum-sucking pig! You son of a motherless goat! - Lucky Day in Three Amigos! (1986)

Frankly, my dear, I don't give a damn. - Rhett Butler in Gone with the Wind (1939)

Well, it was like when I met your mom, God rest her soul. I didn't have so much as a toilet to clean. Still, I wasn't going to pay her a dime for sex, no matter what she was charging. – Bob Bigalow in Deuce Bigalow: Male Gigolo (1999)

What the fuck; I ain't killed nobody in a long time. – Slammer in I'm Gonna Git You Sucka (1988)

You know his name... The Princess Bride (1987)

Hello. My name is Inigo Montoya. You killed my father. Prepare to die. – Inigo in The Princess Bride (1987)

Holy hell son, you're about as useful as a cock flavored lollypop. Dodgeball: – Patches O'Houlihan in A True Underdog Story (2004)

If I had a dog with a face like yours I'd shave his ass and teach him to walk backwards. – Brain Kelly in Gleaming the Cube (1989)

General Zod does not take orders. He gives them. – Ursa in Superman II (1980)

Kick his ass Seabass! - Dumb and Dumber (1994)

Yeah, well, it's a good thing you're not stacked, Harry, or I'd be banging you right now. I'd show you what a real man can do. Split you like an old piece of firewood. You'd probably like it too, you big homo... Don't tell me to shut up woman! – Lloyd Christmas in Dumb and Dumber (1994)

You pompous, stuck up, snot nosed, English, giant, twerp, scumbag, fuck-face, dickhead, asshole. – Otto in A Fish Called Wanda (1988)

I despise your masquerade; the dishonest way you pose yourself. You and your whole fucking family. - Senator Pat Geary in The Godfather Part II (1974)

Han Solo trying to hook up in The Empire Strikes Back (1980)

Why, you stuck up, half-witted, scruffy-looking Nerf herder. - Princess Leia in Star Wars: Episode V - The Empire Strikes Back (1980)

You stupid fucking cunt. You, Williamson, I'm talking to you, shithead. You just cost me six thousand dollars. Six thousand dollars and one Cadillac. That's right. What are you going to do about it? What are you going to do about it, asshole? You're fucking shit. Where did you learn your trade, you stupid fucking cunt, you idiot? Whoever told you that you could work with men? – Ricky Roma in Glengarry Glen Ross (1992)

It's like killing roaches - you have to kill 'em all, otherwise what's the use? – Paul Kersey in Death Wish 3 (1985)

Listen to me here! You ain't got nothin' on me, nothin'!
You're just a cop! Fuck you and your family! - Al Capone in
The Untouchables (1987)

I want you to get this fuck where he
breathes! I want you to find this nancy-
boy Eliot Ness, I want him dead! I want his
family dead! I want his house burned to
the ground! I wanna go there in the middle
of the night and I wanna piss on his
ashes! - Al Capone in The Untouchables
(1987)

Shut that cunts mouth or I'll come over
there and fuck start her head! – Parker in
The Way of the Gun (2000)

It's a Sicilian message. It means Luca
Brasi sleeps with the fishes. – Clemenza in
The Godfather (1972)

He thinks he's bad and ain't got no class! I'm gonna wrap this shotgun up his muthafuckin' ass! – Dolemite in The Human Tornado (1976)

I can lay you out and fill your mouth with your mother's feces, or we can talk? – Lucifer in The Prophecy (1995)

You shit kicking, stinky, horse manure smelling motherfucker you. You fuck me up over there; I'll stick you in a hole in the fucking desert. - Nicky Santoro in Casino (1995)

My prediction?...Pain. - Clubber Lang in Rocky III (1982)

I'm gonna torture him. I'm gonna crucify him. Real bad. – Clubber Lang In Rocky III (1982)

I live to see you eat that contract, but I hope you leave enough room for my fist because I'm going to ram it into your stomach and break your god-damn spine! - Ben Richards in The Running Man (1987)

You're okay. This one: real fuckin' ugly. – They Live (1988)

You know, you look like your head fell in the cheese dip back in 1957. - Nada in They Live (1988)

So, it's just you 57 cops against KUNG FU JOE? Master of Kung Fu, Karate, Jiu-Jitsu, and all kinds of other shit you ain't never heard of! - Kung Fu Joe in I'm Gonna Git You Sucka (1988)

Don't you think I realize what's going on here, miss? Who do you think I am, huh? Don't you think I know that if I was some hotshot from out of town that pulled inside here and you guys made a reservation mistake, I'd be the first one to get a room and I'd be upstairs relaxing right now. But I'm not some hotshot from out of town, I'm a small reporter from "Rolling Stone" magazine that's in town to do an exclusive interview with Michael Jackson that's gonna be picked up by every major magazine in the country. I was gonna call the article "Michael Jackson Is Sitting On Top of the World," but now I think I might as well just call it "Michael Jackson Can Sit On Top of the World Just As Long As He Doesn't Sit in the Beverly Palm Hotel 'Cause There's No Niggers Allowed in There!" – Axel Foley in Beverly Hills Cop (1984)

Excuse me, did I hear the f-word out of you? You say fuck again and I'll bang you right to fuck. Now get the fuck out of here. – Ford in The Adventures of Ford Fairlane (1990)

Why did you stop hooking? You had your future pretty well mapped out for yourself. - Zack Carey in Showgirls (1995)

Ladies and gentlemen, welcome to my underground lair. I have gathered here before me the world's deadliest assassins, and yet each of you has failed to kill Austin Powers. That makes me angry. And when Dr. Evil gets angry, Mr. Bigglesworth gets upset. And when Mr. Bigglesworth gets upset... People die! – Dr. Evil in Austin Powers: International Man of Mystery (1997)

I am the devil, and I am here to do the devil's work. - Otis Driftwood in The Devil's Rejects (2005)

You ever listen to K-Billy's Super Sounds of the Seventies weekend? It's my personal favorite. - Mr. Blonde in Reservoir Dogs (1992)

Are you gonna bark all day little doggie? Or are you gonna bite? - Mr. Blonde in Reservoir Dogs (1992)

I'm stuck in this pit, working for less than slave wages. Working on my day off, the goddamn steel shutters are closed, I deal with every backward ass fuck on the planet. I smell like shoe polish. My ex-girlfriend is catatonic after fucking a dead guy. And my present girlfriend has sucked 36 dicks. – Dante in Clerks (1994)

Mr. Madison, what you've just said is one of the most insanely idiotic things I have ever heard. At no point in your rambling, incoherent response were you even close to anything that could be considered a rational thought. Everyone in this room is now dumber for having listened to it. I award you no points, and may God have mercy on your soul. – The Principal in Billy Madison (1995)

I walk into someone's place of work, they shit scared. They know I'm not a cop, think I've come to kill 'em. And I would. I'll kill anybody who crosses me. Know what I mean? – Lite in Repo Man (1984)

I'll be back. – The Terminator in The Terminator (1984)

Lick my plate, you dog dick! – Chop Top The Texas Chainsaw Massacre 2 (1986)

Shut up and send me more pigs to kill! – Wardaddy in Fury (2014)

Callahan is about to make our day in Dirty Harry (1971)

I know what you're thinking, punk. You're thinking, "Did he fire six shots or only five?" Now to tell you the truth I forgot myself in all this excitement. But being this is a .44 Magnum, the most powerful handgun in the world and will blow you head clean off, you've gotta ask yourself a question: "Do I feel lucky?" Well, do ya, punk? - Harry Callahan in Dirty Harry (1971)

Ah, so you and your mom are both wacked? – Jeff in Hard Candy (2005)

I've seen better tennis playing in a tampon commercial. - Helen's Stepson in Bridesmaids (2011)

When you join my command, you take on debit. A debit you owe me personally. Each and every man under my command owes me one hundred Nazi scalps. And I want my scalps. And all y'all will get me one hundred Nazi scalps, taken from the heads of one hundred dead Nazis. Or you will die trying. - Lt. Aldo Raine in Inglourious Basterds (2009)

I bet you're the kind of guy who would fuck a person in the ass and not even have the goddamn common courtesy to give him a reach-around. - Gunnery Sergeant Hartman in Full Metal Jacket (1987)

Showing off his war face in Full Metal Jacket (1987)

You made a big mistake, Matthews. Never scratch dry shit! – Blade in Eye of the Tiger (1986)

I want Hatcher dead. I want his family dead. And if you can't kill him, I'll go kill him, and then I'm gonna kill you. – Screwface in Marked for Death (1990)

Fat, drunk and stupid is no way to go through life, son. - Dean Vernon Wormer in Animal House (1978)

I asked you three times if Delmar Berry lives here? First Blood (1982)

I could have killed 'em all, I could've killed you. In town you're the law, out here it's me. Don't push it! Don't push it or I'll give you a war you won't believe. Let it go. Let it go! – John Rambo in First Blood (1982)

You know, I'd almost forgotten what your eyes looked like. Still the same. Pissholes in the snow. - Jack Carter in Get Carter (1971)

Keep your money. You just get that sucker to the designated place at the designated time, and I will gladly designate his ass... for dismemberment! - Sho'nuff in The Last Dragon (1985)

Hey dirtbag, you're a lousy shot. I don't like lousy shots. You wasted a kid and now... Now I think it's time to waste you. - Marion Cobretti in Cobra (1986)

Put the knife away, kid, or I'll use it to cut welfare checks from your rotten skin. – Hobo in Hobo with a Shotgun (2011)

He's dead now. He's dead because Mommy killed him. –
Marge (Creepy Mom) in A Nightmare on Elm Street (1984)

I'm your boyfriend now, Nancy. – Fred Krueger in A Nightmare on Elm Street (1984)

It's conceivable, you miserable, vomitous mass, that I'm only lying here because I lack the strength to stand. But, then again... perhaps I have the strength after all. – Westley in The Princess Bride (1987)

You know what I am? I'm your worst fucking nightmare, man. I'm a nigger with a badge which means I got permission to kick your fucking ass whenever I feel like it! – Reggie Hammond in 48 Hrs. (1982)

Gentlemen, Chicolini here may talk like an idiot, and look like an idiot, but don't let that fool you: he really is an idiot. - Rufus T. Firefly in Duck Soup (1933)

Get this through your head you Jew motherfucker, you. You only exist out here because of me. That's the only reason. Without me, you, personally, every fucking wise guy skell around will take a piece of your fucking Jew ass. Then where you gonna go? You're fucking warned. Don't ever go over my fucking head again. You motherfucker, you. - Nicky Santoro in Casino (1995)

I will be watching you and if I find that you are trying to corrupt my first born child, I will bring you down, baby. I will bring you down to Chinatown. - Jack Byrnes in Meet the Parents (2000)

The top five Chuck Norris insults and threats that kick ass:

5. See, you ain't nothing but a chicken shit pussy asshole who lives on the misery and suffering of others. And when it comes for you, you'll be crying like a baby. - Colonel Scot McCoy in Delta Force 2: The Colombian Connection (1990)

4. My kind of trouble doesn't take vacations. – J.J. McQuade in Lone Wolf McQuade (1983)

3. When I want your opinion, I'll beat it out of you. – Eddie Cusack in Code of Silence (1985)

2. One night you'll close your eyes, and when they open I'll be there. It'll be time to die. – Matt Hunter in Invasion U.S.A. (1985)

1. I don't step on toes, Littlejohn, I step on necks. - Colonel James Braddock in Braddock: Missing in Action III (1988)

<u>Runner Up Quote:</u> Sleep tight, sucker. - Major Scott McCoy The Delta Force (1986)

Reggie, your breathe is so stinky people look forward to your farts. - Buddy Love in The Nutty Professor (1996)

Zod arrives on the planet Houston in Superman II (1980)

I am General Zod. Your ruler. Yes, today begins a new order. Your lands, your possessions, your very lives, will gladly be given in tribute to me, General Zod! In return for your obedience you will enjoy my generous protection. In other words you will be allowed to live. – General Zod in Superman II (1980)

I will kill you when I am ready. Be it next week, next month perhaps next year. But first, I'm going to make you suffer in the same way you made me suffer! - Edward Lionheart in Theatre of Blood (1973)

Aww, you motherfuckers. Okay. Alright. I'm putting cases on all you bitches. Huh. You think you can do this shit... Jake. You think you can do this to me? You motherfuckers will be playing basketball in Pelican Bay when I get finished with you. SHU program nigga. 23 hour lockdown. I'm the man up in this piece. You'll never see the light of...Who the fuck do you think you're fucking  with? I'm the police, I run shit around here! You just live here. Yeah, that's right, you better walk away. Go on and walk away... 'cause I'm gonna' burn this motherfucker down. King Kong ain't got shit on me. - Alonzo Harris in Training Day (2001)

Oh, that's funny to you? You won't be laughing when someone prematurely pops in your face. It stings. And that is now why I have a lazy eye. - Gary in Old School (2003)

Now let's see if you can defend yourself, you sweat from a baboon's balls. – Semmi in Coming to America (1988)

Yippee-ki-yay, motherfucker. – John McClane in Die Hard (1988)

You want to spit on me and make me crawl? I'm gonna piss on your grave tomorrow. Pam Grier in Coffy (1973)

This is the end of your rotten life, you motherfucking dope pusher! - Coffy in Coffy (1973)

You can eat shit as far as I'm concerned, Miss Sandstone, or eat anything you like, or do anything you like, just don't assume that I want to know your troubles. Now if you wouldn't mind, I'm a busy woman with a full day's work ahead of me. Please remove yourself from my office! - Connie Marble in Pink Flamingos (1972)

Bruce flexing on a purse snatcher in a classic scene. They Call Me Bruce (1982)

With my right foot I can knock out that knife. With my left I can kick your nose. With this hand I can poke out your eyes. With this I can break your neck. Take a good look at my face, I'm an Oriental. – Bruce in They Call me Bruce? (1982)

Maybe I'm just not making myself clear. I don't want to fuck with you, Sal. But I got the connections. I got the sales organization. I got the muscle to shove enough of this factory so far up your stupid wop ass that you'll shit snow for a year. - Clarence Boddicker in Robocop (1987)

I knew you were up to something, though I'll confess I hadn't thought of necrophilia? - Prince Barin in Flash Gordon (1980)

She's not a woman...she's the Terminator.
- Larry in Throw Momma from the Train
(1987)

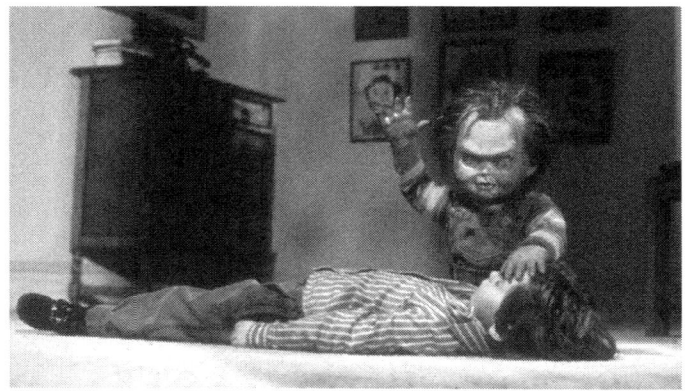

Hi, I'm Chucky, and I'm your friend till the end. Hidey-ho!
Child's Play (1988)

You stupid bitch. You filthy slut. I'll teach
you to fuck with me! – Chucky in Child's
Play (1988)

A census taker once tried to test me. I ate
his liver with some fava beans and a nice
chianti. - Hannibal Lecter in The Silence of
the Lambs (1991)

Shit...You shoot me in a dream, you better
wake up and apologize. – Mr. White in
Reservoir Dogs (1992)

Suck my cock! I'll kill your family! - Jackie
Moon in Semi-Pro (2008)

Every town has a story. Tombstone has a legend.
Tombstone (1993)

You die first, get it? Your friends might get me in a rush, but not before I make your head into a canoe, you understand me? - Wyatt Earp in Tombstone (1993)

I don't know who you are. I don't know what you want. If you are looking for ransom, I can tell you I don't have money. But what I do have are a very particular set of skills, skills I have acquired over a very long career. Skills that make me a nightmare for people like you. If you let my daughter go now, that'll be the end of it. I will not look for you, I will not pursue you. But if you don't, I will look for you, I will find you, and I will kill you. – Bryan Mills in Taken (2008)

I hate all the orphans in the whole world! - Esqueleto in Nacho Libre (2006)

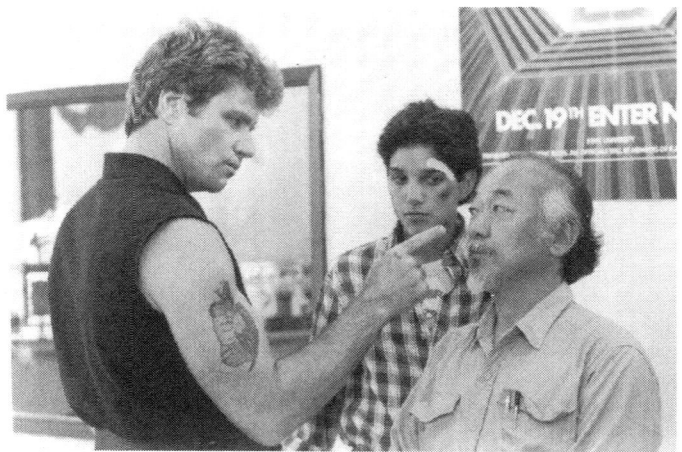

This is a karate dojo, not a knitting class. You don't come into my dojo, drop a challenge and leave, old man. The Karate Kid (1984)

We do not train to be merciful here. Mercy is for the weak. Here, in the streets, in competition: A man confronts you, he is the enemy. An enemy deserves no mercy. - John Kreese in The Karate Kid (1984)

Yeah, well you were the inspiration for twin beds! - Monty Capuletti in Easy Money (1983)

Any of you fucking pricks move, and I'll execute every motherfucking last one of ya! – Honey Bunny in Pulp Fiction (1994)

You better watch what you say about my car. She's real sensitive. - Arnie Cunningham in Christine (1983)

I'm gonna take you to the bank, Senator Trent. To the blood bank! – Mason Storm in Hard To Kill (1990)

How am I gonna get a scar like that eating pussy?
Scarface (1983)

You wanna fuck with me? Okay. You wanna play rough? Okay. Say hello to my little friend! – Tony Montana in Scarface (1983)

I'd like Frank Shirley, my boss, right here tonight. I want him brought from his happy holiday slumber over there on Melody Lane with all the other rich people and I want him brought right here, with a big ribbon on his head, and I want to look him straight in the eye and I want to tell him what a cheap, lying, no-good, rotten, four flushing, low-life, snake licking, dirt eating, inbred, overstuffed, ignorant, blood-sucking, dog kissing, brainless, dickless, hopeless, heartless, fat-ass, bug-eyed, stiff-legged, spotty-lipped, worm-headed sack of monkey shit he is! Hallelujah! Holy shit! - Clark Griswold in Christmas Vacation (1989)

That's not a joke, that's a severe behavioral disorder. I mean, the next thing you know, you'll be wearing a bra on your head! Poor Chet. Weird Science (1985)

Boy, I wouldn't give a squirt of piss for your ass right now. – Chet in Weird Science (1985)

Hey, laser lips! Your mother was a snow blower! – Johnny Number 5 in Short Circuit (1986)

Fuck you, fuckball! - Ray Bones Barboni in Get Shorty (1995)

Who's going to believe a talking head? Get a job in a sideshow. - Herbert West in Re-Animator (1985)

You no-business, born-insecure, junkyard motherfucker! - Dolemite (1974)

Man, move over and let me pass before they have be to pulling these Hush Puppies out your motherfuckin' ass! – Dolemite in Dolemite (1974)

I hate you! You did this to me you miserable piece of dick-brained, horseshit slime-sucking son of a whore bitch! - Gail in Nine Months (1995)

Your mom goes to college. – Kip in Napoleon Dynamite (2004)

I don't want to talk to you no more, you empty headed animal food trough wiper. I fart in your general direction! Your mother was a hamster and your father smelt of elderberries! - French Soldier in Monty Python and the Holy Grail (1975)

You have the manners of a goat and you smell like a dung-heap. And you've no knowledge whatsoever of your potential. Now, get out! – Ramirez in Highlander (1986)

Harry, let's face it. And I'm not being funny. I mean no disrespect, but you're a cunt. You're a cunt now, and you've always been a cunt. And the only thing that's going to change is that you're going to be an even bigger cunt. Maybe have some more cunt kids. – Harry in In Bruges (2008)

I wouldn't let you sleep in my room if you were growing on my ass. - Buzz McCallister in Home Alone (1990)

I'll send you a love letter, straight from my heart, fucker! You know what a love letter is? It's a bullet from a fucking gun, fucker! You receive a love letter from me, you're fucked forever! You understand, fuck? I'll send you straight to hell, fucker! – Frank Booth in Blue Velvet (1986)

Fuckface...I like that one Errol. I'll have to remember that one next time I'm climbing off your mom. – Errol in Snatch. (2000)

Bother me about a steak? - DeNiro in Raging Bull (1980)

This son of a bitch just called me an animal? Hey you, I'm gonna get ahold of that dog and I'm gonna eat it for lunch. You hear what I'm saying? You hear me Larry? Larry?...Who's an animal? Your mothers an animal you son of a bitch. You're gonna find your dog dead in the hallway tomorrow ya bum. – Jake LaMotta in Raging Bull (1980)

Your mom's the one who's embarrassing. What a phony. But, your dad's actually kind of cute. – Angela Hayes in American Beauty (1999)

Two for flinching in Stand By Me (1986)

Why don't you go home and fuck your mother some more? - Chris Chambers in Stand by Me (1986)

Bullshit. It looks to me like the best part of you ran down the crack of your mama's ass and ended up as a brown stain on the mattress. - Gunnery Sergeant Hartman in Full Metal Jacket (1987)

The plan is you drink a nice tall glass of shut the fuck up. - CJ in Dawn of the Dead (2004)

You're a sexist, egotistical, lying, hypocritical bigot...You're foul, Hart. A wart on the nose of humanity and I'm going to blast it off... Goodbye boss man. It's quitting time! – Judy in Nine to Five (1980)

I will fucking cum right on you! I will cum like a fucking madman all over you, McBride! - James Franco in This Is The End (2013)

We've got bush! - Booger in Revenge of the Nerds (1984)

I thought I was looking at my mother's old douchebag but that's in Ohio. – Booger in Revenge of The Nerds (1984)

All you motherfuckers are gonna pay. You are the ones who are the ball-lickers. We're gonna fuck your mothers while you watch and cry like little whiny bitches. Once we get to Hollywood and find those Miramax fucks who is making the movie... we're gonna make them eat our shit, then shit out our shit, and then eat their shit that's made up of our shit that we made 'em eat. Then you're all you motherfucks are next. – Jay from Jay and Silent Bob Strike Back (2001)

You're mother's a tracer! - Banky Edwards in Chasing Amy (1997)

Reggie, I heard of dreadlocks, but shitlocks? That ain't you hair, man. Take that pile of shit off your head! - Poor Reggie getting his balls busted in The Nutty Professor (1996)

Your mother's so fat, the bitch needs Thomas Guide to find her asshole! Alright! Wait, wait, wait, your mother's so fat, after sex I roll over twice, and I'm still on the bitch! Your mother is so fat, she fell in the Grand Canyon and got stuck! Reggie's mother's so fat, that the bitch gets her toenails painted at Earl Scheib! Earl Scheib! At Earl Scheib! – Buddy Love in The Nutty Professor (1996)

Don't fucking scream at me! Look at you! With your fucking 48% body fat! And you, you scrawny little bastard! Fuck you guys! – Breacher in Sabotage (2014)

I will smash your face into a car windshield, and then take your mother Dorothy Mantooth out for a nice seafood dinner and never call her again. – Champ Kind in Anchorman: The Legend of Ron Burgundy (2004)

When you have to shoot, shoot. Don't talk. - Tuco in The Good, the Bad and The Ugly (1996)

You want to know who you are? Huh? You want to know who's son you are? You don't, I do, everybody does...you're the son of a thousand fathers, all bastards like you. – Tuco in The Good, the Bad and the Ugly (1966)

Stand up you scum sucking pig! – Rio in One-Eyed Jacks (1961)

I have come here to chew bubblegum and kick ass... and I'm all out of bubblegum. – Nada in They Live (1988)

Farley and Spade singing Superstar by The Carpenters in Tommy Boy (1995)

No offense, but if I showed a picture of your mom to some of my buddies at school, she'd definitely be 'Boner of the Month'. – Tommy Callahan in Tommy Boy (1995)

All units: Serial Mom is headed South on Ceswick. Proceed with caution. She is armed and fucking nuts! - Cop in Serial Mom (1994)

If I had a nickel for every cigarette your mom smoked, I'd be dead. – Donna in Twin Peaks: Fire Walk with Me (1992)

They can suck my pathetic little dick, and I'll dip my nuts in marinara sauce just so the fat bastards can get a taste of home while they're at it. - Rocco in The Boondock Saints (1999)

Hey, Boris. What would you do if I told you your pinko Commie mother sucked so much dick, her face looks like an egg? – Rocco in The Boondock Saints (1999)

The next time you point a gun at me, you better pull that trigger, because I'm going to blow you into so many pieces your friends will get tired of looking for you. - Matt Fletcher in The Appaloosa (1966)

Shit eating son of a bitch! Bastard, douche bag, twat, numb-nuts, dickhead, Bitch! - Bob Wiley in What About Bob? (1991)

You know how I know you're gay? You have a rainbow bumper sticker on your car that says "I love it when balls are in my face." - David in The 40-Year Old Virgin (2005)

Ana waking up to the worst day ever in Dawn of the Dead (2004)

Bart, dude, everybody's dead, okay? Your mom's dead. Your brother's dead. That fat chick at Dairy Queen? Dead! – Terry in Dawn of the Dead (2004)

Tell you what to do...Take her to the zoo. I hear retards like the zoo. – Bodyguard in Rocky (1976)

My mom's been fuckin' a dead guy for 30 years. I call him dad. - Randal in Clerks (1994)

Your slut mother was fucking my father. She's the reason my mom moved out and abandoned me. How's that for a motive? – Billy in Scream (1996)

We have an unusual problem here, Jane. You obviously want me dead, and I'm less and less concerned for your well-being. – John Smith in Mr. & Mrs. Smith (2005)

Chazz Reinhold, making the move to funerals in The Wedding Crashers (2005)

Hey mom, can we get some meat loaf? What is she doing back there? I never know what she's doing...Mom! The meat loaf! Fuck! - Chazz Reinhold in Wedding Crashers (2005)

I'm going to impale your mom on a spike and feed her dead body to my dog with syphilis. – Jack in Thank You for Smoking (2005)

You know what, I'll ask your mom to read it for me next time I got her bent over the console. – Lustig in Devil (2010)

Silly Caucasian girl likes to play with Samurai swords.. The Bride in Kill Bill Vol. 1 (2003)

It was not my intention to do this in front of you. For that I'm sorry. But you can take my word for it, your mother had it coming. When you grow up, if you still feel raw about it, I'll be waiting. – The Bride in Kill Bill: Vol. 1 (2003)

Hey baby you're alright. You must have been something before electricity? - Al Czervik in Caddyshack (1980)

I'll shove that bat up your ass and turn you into a popsicle - Ajax in The Warriors (1979)

Robyn wouldn't piss on your gums if your teeth were on fire. – Matt in Encino Man (1992)

The top five worst things said about someone's adoring mother in a movie:

5. You know the difference between your Mom and washing machine? When I dump a load in the washing machine it doesn't follow me around for three weeks. - Cam Brady in The Campaign (2012)

4. Stop crying, you sniveling ass! Stop your nonsense. You're just the afterbirth, Eli, slithered out on your mother's filth...They should have put you in glass jar on a mantelpiece. – Daniel Plainview in There Will Be Blood (2007)

3. You listening? Your mother sucks fucking big fucking elephant dicks. Got that? – Joey in Raging Bull (1980)

2. Your mother's cunt stinks like carpet cleaner. - Henry in Barfly (1987)

1. Your mother sucks cocks in Hell, Karras, you faithless slime. – Demon in Regan in The Exorcist (1973)

I married your mother because I wanted children. Imagine my disappointment when you arrived. - Professor Wagstaff in Horse Feathers (1932)

Yeah, but Richie ain't here! Know why? Cause he's a chicken shit fucking pussy asshole! - Detective Gino Felino NYPD in Out For Justice (1991)

All we got on this team are a bunch of Jews, spics, niggers, pansies, and a booger-eating moron! - Tanner Boyle in The Bad News Bears (1976)

I would tell you to kiss my ass too, but you probably can't find it, you blind motherfucker! - Vera in Harlem Nights (1989)

Sergeant, you get that contraband stogie out of my face before I shove it so far up your ass you'll have to set fire to your nose to light it. - Highway in Heartbreak Ridge (1986)

I'm gonna put a bullet hole in your fucking forehead, and I'm gonna fuck the brain hole! - Mr. Grocer in Grosse Pointe Blank (1997)

Walk's like a black man, breathes like a killer. – Dinky-D in Today You Die (2005)

You cock juggling thunder cunt! - Hannibal in Blade Trinity (2004)

My love for you is like a truck, Berzerker! Would you like some making fuck, Berzerker! - Olaf Oleeson in Clerks (1994)

You're the problem! You're the fucking problem you fucking Dr. White honkin' jam-rag fucking spunk-bubble! - Don Logan in Sexy Beast (2000)

To everyone here who matters, you're vapor, you're spam, a waste of perfectly good yearbook space, and nothing's ever gonna change that. - Taylor in She's All That (1999)

I think you are filth. I think you are scum! You are a degenerate! - Mr. Robinson in The Graduate (1967)

I don't deal with psychos. I put them away. - Stallone as Marion Cobretti in Cobra (1986)

You're the disease, and I'm the cure. - Marion Cobretti in Cobra (1986)

He's a pedantic, pontificating, pretentious bastard, a belligerent old fart, a worthless steaming pile of cow dung, figuratively speaking. - Fletcher in Liar Liar (1997)

So there you are, tubby. Look like a bucket of lard on a bad day. You baby gorilla. Why don't you work in a zoo, and stop bothering people? I got a call yesterday from Baskin Robbins, they said that they're down to only five flavors. You're swelling up as I talk to you. - Mr. Hamilton in Dirty Work (1998)

Don't move, dirtbag! - Cadet Laverne Hooks in Police Academy (1984)

You eat when we say you eat. You piss when we say you piss, and you shit when we say you shit. You got that, you maggot dick motherfucker? - The charming Captain Hadley in The Shawshank Redemption (1994)

Isn't that just like a wop. Brings a knife to a gun fight. Get outta here you Dago Bastard! Go on get your ass outta here! - Malone in The Untouchables (1987)

I wouldn't live with you if the world were flooded with piss and you lived in a tree. - Julie Buckman in Parenthood (1989)

You know Spider, you're a fucking mumbling stuttering little fuck. You know that? – Tommy DeVito in Goodfellas (1990)

We came, we saw, we kicked its ass! - The team saving the day in Ghostbusters (1984)

Yes it's true. This man has no dick - Dr. Peter Venkman in Ghostbusters (1984)

Now, Samantha, all I said was your breath smells like you've been drinking out of Ms. Mackinaw's douche bag, that's all. - Heather in The Woods (2006)

I've heard better singing from a mongoose with throat cancer! - Trevor in Meet the Feebles (1989)

To call you stupid would be an insult to stupid people. I've known sheep who could outwit you. I've worn dresses with higher IQs, but you think you're an intellectual, don't you, ape? You know what you are? Just a dirty son of a bitch! - Wanda Gershwitz in A Fish Called Wanda (1988)

Murdock...I'm coming to get you! John Rambo in Rambo First Blood Part 2 (1985)

Black, bold and bloody mean! Isaac Hayes is Mac 'Truck' Turner (1974)

Those two bitches that left - they had better learn to sell pussy in Iceland because if I ever see them again, I'm gonna cut their fucking throats! - Dorinda in Truck Turner (1974)

I've done far worse than kill you, Admiral. I've hurt you. And I wish to go on hurting you. I shall leave you as you left me, as you left her; marooned for all eternity in the center of a dead planet... buried alive! Buried alive! – Khan in Star Trek II: The Wrath of Khan (1982)

Hey, what do you like, the leg or the wing, Henry? Or ya still go for the old hearts and lungs? - Joe Pesci as Tommy DeVito in Goodfellas (1990)

Tommy, if I was gonna break your balls I'd tell you to go home and get your shine box. - Billy Batts in Goodfellas (1990)

You can all me father, you can call me Jacob, you can call me Jake, you can call me a dirty son of a bitch. But if you ever call me daddy again I'll finish this fight. - Jacaob McCandles in Big Jake (1971)

Sit your five dollar ass down before I make change. - Nino Brown in New Jack City (1991)

I told you not to be stupid, you moron. – Ben Stern in Private Parts (1997)

Dear Darla, I hate your stinking guts. You make me vomit. You're scum between my toes! Love, Alfalfa. – Buckwheat (reading a letter) in The Little Rascals (1994)

I once thought I had mono for an entire year. It turned out I was just really bored. - Wayne Campbell in Wayne's World (1992)

Benjamin is nobody's friend. If Benjamin were an ice cream flavor, he'd be pralines and dick. - Garth in Wayne's World (1992)

You always were a problem for me, Joey. When Mom brought you home from the hospital, I tried to strangle you in your crib. - Richie Cusack in A History in Violence (2005)

You're one ugly motherfucker. - Dutch in Predator (1987)

That's angel food cake. You touch her and the Food and Drug Administration will get you for fucking food. - Coach Brakett in Porky's (1982)

Life, liberty and the pursuit of vengeance. Jamie Foxx in Django Unchained (2012)

Kill white people and get paid for it? What's not to like? - Django in Django Unchained (2012)

You want freedom? I'll give you fucking freedom. You're going to jail, faggot. How's that for freedom? Freedom to get fucked up the ass by some big buck nigger. Give me your other hand! He's gonna be right behind you. Just like this. You're gonna like that, won't you, you faggot fuck? - Nick The Nazi Army Surplus Store owner in Falling Down (1993)

Vincent Van Gogh. Everyone said to him, "You can't be a great painter, you only have one ear." And you know what he said? "I can't hear you." – Dinner for Schmucks (2010)

I know that you take a magic marker and draw a face on your penis and you put a little hat on it and you call it Sammy. Then you sing to it...Ahhh ahhh ahhh - Barry in Dinner for Schmucks (2010)

How would you like to bite that in the butt, develop lockjaw, and be dragged to death? – Dakota in Lone Wolf McQuade (1983)

I knew it. I'm surrounded by assholes! – Dark Helmet in Spaceballs (1987)

Lucky? You wanna talk about luck? You're fucking lucky the toilet wouldn't flush when your mom spread her legs and pulled you out with a goddamned coat hanger. – Joey in Gutterballs (2008)

Fuck you! You need to shut the fuck up 'cause without that badge and gun, you ain't shit! You're less than motherfucking nothing. You motherfucking border hopping, donkey riding Mexican motherfucker. - Mr. Tre in End of Watch (2012)

Kiss my sweaty balls you fat fuck! - Malcolm Tucker in In The Loop (2009)

I will fucking massacre you! – Lee Grossmann freaking the fuck out in Tropic Thunder (2008)

Ok, Flaming Dragon..fuckface. First, take a big step back and literally fuck your own face! - Les Grossman in Tropic Thunder (2008)

Come on Bennett, put away that chicken shit gun. You don't just want to pull a trigger. Put the knife in me! – Matrix in Commando (1985)

Sorry, folks! We're closed for two weeks to clean and repair America's favorite family fun park. Sorry, uh-huh, uh-huh, uh-huh! – Marty the Moose's last words in National Lampoon's Vacation (1983)

I think you're all fucked in the head. We're ten hours from the fucking fun park and you want to bail out? Well I'll tell you something, this is no longer a vacation. It's a quest. It's a quest for fun. I'm gonna have fun and you're gonna have fun. We're all gonna have so much fucking fun we'll need plastic surgery to remove our goddamn smiles. You'll be whistling 'Zip-A-Dee-Doo-Dah' out of your assholes! I gotta be crazy! I'm on a pilgrimage to see a moose. Praise Marty Moose! Holy shit! - National Lampoon's Vacation (1983)

Shut up and sit down, you big, bald fuck. - Avi in Snatch (2000)

Fool! Your fare is the only thing stopping me from breaking your face! – Samson in D.C. Cab (1983)

Dead Mike, Stab Master Arson and MC Gusto busting rhymes Straight Outta Locash in CB4 (1993)

Turn around and eat your big ass biscuit! – Euripides in CB4 (1993)

Watch this motherfucker! Watch this you cocksucker! Look at that! You can't do a thing about that can you? Can you? Look at me! Can you? Can you fuckface? Can you? There, move. Move you cocksucker. Move. I'd like to blow your fucking face apart. - The Lieutenant in Bad Lieutenant (1992)

When they bleached your hair, they must have bleached your brain too. - Charles Tatum in Ace in the Hole (1951)

Look at me! I was gonna be a stand-up comedian! Who's gonna laugh now? – Cherry Darling in Planet Terror (2007)

I've seen me a lot of weird shit in my day, but I ain't never seen a one-legged stripper. I seen me a stripper with one breast. And I seen me a stripper with twelve toes. I've even seen me a stripper with no brains at all, but I ain't never seen a one-legged stripper and I've been to Morocco. - The Rapist in Planet Terror (2007)

Your mother was my favorite whore in Marrakech. Man, she knew how to polish a helmet! – Swan in Escape Plan (2013)

I swear, I'm so pissed off at my mom. As soon as she's of age, I'm putting her in a home. - Brennan Huff in Step Brothers (2008)

Stupid fucking idiot! Red-shirted ass. You guys think you're so fucking cool, it makes me sick! "Oh, let's go make fun of the vegans, and their crazy lifestyle!" We're not hurting anyone! Go eat a hamburger and choke on a cow dick! – Shiloh in Grandma's Boy (2006)

Will you just say something bad you fucking Quaker? - Guy Trilby in Bad Words (2013)

Why don't you take your potty mouth, go locate your pre-teen cock-sucking son and stuff him back up that old blown-out sweat sock of a vagina and scoot off back to whatever shit-kicking town you came from! - Guy Trilby in Bad Words (2013)

I call that bold talk for a one eyed fat man.- Ned Pepper in True Grit (1969)

If it wasn't for me, you'd still be slinging hash in that shithouse and fucking your boss. – Ed Wilson in Natural Born Killers (1994)

What do you think this is the Army, where you shoot 'em a mile away? You've gotta get up close like this and BADA-BING! You blow their brains all over your nice Ivy League suit. Come here, you're taking this very personal. Tom, this is business and this man is taking it very, very personal. - Sonny Corleone in The Godfather (1972)

Why me Lord? You made other men out of clay. Mine, you made out of shit. – Cholla in Any Which Way You Can (1980)

Though I walk through the valley of the shadow of death, I will chew on Philo Beddoe's ass for my last supper! - Cholla, Leader of The Black Widows in Any Which Way You Can (1980)

The top five memorable dick insults that make me laugh every time I hear them:

5. If I had a dick this is where I'd tell you to suck it. - Mrs. Bickerman in Lake Placid (1999)

4. I'd tell you to blow it out your ass, but my dick's in the way. - Stacy in The Limey (1999)

3. You're gonna look real funny sucking my dick with no teeth. - Captain Hadley in The Shawshank Redemption (1994)

2. Hey, try not to suck any dick on the way through the parking lot. – Dante in Clerks (1994)

1. I don't care if you wake up in a ditch with grown men shitting on you and jumping on top of your head. Maybe your nose will turn into a big ole dick and you can stroke that all the time. I hope your hair turns into dog shit one day. You wake up and you run your comb through it and all that it is, is little trundles of dog shit. The worst shit that you could imagine. AIDS... it's cool. Everything comes around sweetheart. – Fred Simmons in The Foot Fist Way (2006)

You touch my brother with that stake biker, and vampires won't have to suck your blood. They'll be able to lick it up off the floor. - Seth in From Dusk Till Dawn (1996)

In my experience, Nick, lessons not learned in blood are soon forgotten. - Clyde Shelton in Law Abiding Citizen (2009)

I'm just getting warmed up. This is von Clausewitz shit. Total fucking war. I'm gonna pull the whole thing down. I'm gonna bring the whole fucking diseased, corrupt temple down on your head. It's gonna be biblical. - Clyde Shelton in Law Abiding Citizen (2009)

Spartans! Ready your breakfast and eat hearty. For tonight, we dine in hell! - Spartan King Leonidas to troops in 300 (2006)

You're gonna wish you never fucking got up this fucking morning asshole, because my boyfriend's gonna fuck you up! And then after that while he's fucking up your fucking gay uncle over there I'm gonna fucking cut off your cock and mail it to your mother, you fucking faggot bitch! You gaylord fucking bitch! How do you like that? You like that a lot you fucking faggot? You like to ass fuck? Fontanella fucking babyheads! - Raving Bitch in The Way of the Gun (2000)

You look like a grown-up version of Bam-Bam. - Ice busting Joe Huff's balls in Stone Cold (1991)

Imagine the future, Chains, 'cause you're not in it. - Joe Huff in Stone Cold (1991)

Stay gold, Ponyboy. Stay gold. – Johnny in The Outsiders (1983)

**That's my puck, baby, don't you ever touch my puck. –
Happy in Happy Gilmore (1996)**

You can trouble me for a warm glass of
shut the hell up! Now, you will go to sleep!
Or, I will put you to sleep. Check out the
name tag. You're in my world now,
grandma! - Nursing Home Orderly in
Happy Gilmore (1996)

Hey, look. I'm sorry I made you clean the
toilets and the bathtubs, I mean, who did
all the work in bed? - Ford in The
Adventures of Ford Fairlane (1990)

I'm going to kill you and fuck you at the
same time! - Cappy Capulet in Tromeo
and Juliet (1996)

It's 106 miles to Chicago, we got a full
tank of gas, half a pack of cigarettes, it's
dark... and we're wearing sunglasses. –
Elwood in The Blues Brothers (1980)

I'm sorry to disappoint you but you're gonna live to enjoy all the glorious fruits life has got to offer - Acne, shaving, premature ejaculation...and your first divorce. – Jack Slater in The Last Action Hero (1993)

Hey, you wanna be a farmer? Here's a couple of achers! - Jack Slater in The Last Action Hero (1993)

I will kill you when I am ready. Be it next week, next month perhaps next year. But first, I'm going to make you suffer in the same way you made me suffer! - Edward Lionheart Theatre of Blood (1973)

That's all you got, lady. Two wrong feet in fucking ugly shoes. - Erin in Erin Brockovich (2000)

Look at those assholes, ordinary fucking people. I hate 'em. – Bud in Repo Man (1984)

Let me tell you something, pendejo. You pull any of your crazy shit with us, you flash a piece out on the lanes, I'll take it away from you, stick it up your ass and pull the fucking trigger 'til it goes click. - Jesus Quintana in The Big Lebowski (1998)

First you gotta do the truffle shuffle. – Mouth in The Goonies (1985)

I'm gonna hit you so hard that when you wake up your clothes will be out of style! - Brandon Walsh in The Goonies (1985)

Welcome, whores of Salem! I can taste the foul stench of your ancestors rotting in the folds of filth between your legs! - Margaret Morgan in Lords of Salem (2012)

I'm the guy that put the bathrooms in this joint. That's who I am. – Nicky in Easy Money (1983)

My mother-in-law, for years I wouldn't kiss her face; I end up kissing her ass! - Monty Capuletti in Easy Money (1983)

I saw the way your friend Mauricio looked at me; I thought he was going to shoot me with a tranquilizer gun and tag my ear. – Rosemary in Shallow Hal (2001)

You two legged yellow dog, that's what you are. Come on shoot me! Shoot me! But I'll tell you something Mr. Poor White Trash, you aint nothing but what you got in your hand. And your pappy should have thought about that before he stuck it in your mammy! - Grandma Turner in Fight for Your Life (1977)

You just made the biggest mistake of your life, baby. I know you're gonna be missing me when you have that big, white, wrinkly body on you with his loose skin and old balls... gross! Ugh! - Sonny in Big Daddy (1999)

Do what? Do I ice her? Do I marry her? Which one of these? - Charley Partanna in Prizzi's Honor (1985)

If Marxie Heller was so fucking smart, how come he's so fucking dead? - Charley Partanna in Prizzi's Honor (1985)

From what I hear, you couldn't hit water if you fell out of a fucking boat. - Crash Davis in Bull Durham (1988)

One hundred thousand sperm and you were the fastest? - Cyril Bench in Vertical Limit (2000)

I will bitch-slap you back to Africa. - Chief Inspector Lee in Rush Hour 2 (2001)

Bring out the Gimp. – Zed in Pulp Fiction (1994)

You lousy cork-soakers. You have violated my farging rights. – Roman Moronie before being deported to Sweden in Johnny Dangerously (1984)

You farging sneaky bastage. I'm gonna take your dwork. I'm gonna nail it to the wall. I'm gonna crush your boils in a meat grinder. I'm gonna cut off your arms. I'm gonna shove 'em up your icehole. Dirty son-a-ma-batches. My own club! - Roman Moronie in Johnny Dangerously (1984)

Lizards? Who you calling lizards? Your mother was a lizard! – Rool in Willow (1988)

You don't wanna get mixed up with a guy like me. I'm a loner, Dottie. A rebel. – Peewee Herman in Pee-wee's Big Adventure (1985)

I say we stomp him! Then we tattoo him! Then we hang him...and then we kill him! – Biker in Pee-wee's Big Adventure (1985)

This is Rico speaking. Rico! R-I-C-O! Rico! Little Caesar, that's who! You're a big guy just shooting your mouth off for the papers? Well listen, you crummy, flat-footed copper, I'll show you whether I've lost my nerve and my brains! – Rico in Little Caesar (1931)

You get the fuck out of my building. Doug get him out of here. You blow dried jerk mother fucker. Take him out of here and throw him in the incinerator, cut him to little pieces and feed him to the animals out there. Get out of here. - Larry Flynt in The People vs. Larry Flynt (1996)

Happy? Why, I'm so happy I'd like to go up and bust someone in the nose! - Joe Krozac in The Last Gangster (1937)

My first crush was Jaime Lee Curtis in Trading Places (1983)

Cause I'm a karate man! And a karate man bruises on the inside. They don't show their weakness, but you don't know that because you're a big Barry White looking motherfucker! - Billy Ray Valentine in Trading Places (1983)

I'll shut the door on you. You lay down here and put your head in the door. And I'll slam it about 157,000 times. - Mullins in The Heat (2013)

I'm gonna rip your head off and shit down your neck! - Teddy in Stand By Me (1986)

They took your wife away in a balloon? Well you don't need the police, pal, you need a psychiatrist! - Curtis Mooney in Killer Klowns from Outer Space (1988)

Come here honey loosen up will ya? You're a lot of woman, you know that? Hey, you wanna make fourteen dollars the hard way? - Al Czervik in Caddyshack (1980)

Now, if that's a fact, tell me, am I lying? 'Cause you, you're part eggplant... - Clifford Worley in True Romance (1993)

I haven't killed anybody since 1984. Goddamn his soul to burn for eternity in fucking hell for making me get my hands dirty. Go over to this comedian's son's apartment, come back with something that tells me where that asshole went, so I can wipe this egg off my face and finish this fucked-up family for good. – Coccotti in True Romance (1993)

I'm reloaded! Okay? Come on in here, you motherfuckers! Come on, I'm waiting for ya! What, you ain't coming' in? Okay, I'm coming' out! Oh, you up against me now, motherfuckers! I'm gonna blow your fucking brains out! You think you're big time? You gonna fucking die big time! You ready? Here comes the pain! - Carlito Brigante in Carlito's Way (1993)

Big round of applauds for Jackson Heights own, Mr. Randy Watson, Yes! Randy Watson! - Rev. Brown introducing Sexual Chocolate in Coming to America (1988)

I'm warning you. I will be forced to thrash you. - Prince Akeem in Coming to America (1988)

First you rip me off, then you set up Carl, now you want to fuck my lady? - Eric 'Rick' Masters in To Live and Die in L.A. (1985)

Hey, you try making love to a complete stranger in a hostile, mutant environment, see how you like it. - Sam Hell in Hell Comes to Frogtown (1988)

You got white shit all over your mouth, Franco. You probably sucked somebody's dick. Jonah over here probably watched and jerked off. – Danny McBride in This is the End (2013)

Hey! Hey, asshole! Hey, come on! Pickle dick, demonic-looking motherfucker. Nobody's scared of you. You ain't a raccoon. Yeah, bring your ass, bitch. Nobody's scared of you. I'm Craig fucking Robinson! Yeah! I hope you like big dick, motherfucker, 'cause, I'm about to fuck you raw. For the last goddamn time! Take your panties off! - Craig Robinson in This is the End (2013)

This town needs an enema! – The Joker in Batman (1989)

Five months in Vietnam, and my best friend is a V.C. This will not look good on my resume! - Adrian Cronauer in Good Morning, Vietnam (1987)

You are in more dire need of a blowjob than any white man in history. - Adrian Cronauer in Good Morning, Vietnam (1987)

You two are the most fucked up people I've ever met and I deal with fucked up people for a living. - Tanner Bolt in Gone Girl (2014)

To crush your enemies, to see them driven before you, and to hear the lamentations of their women. – Conan in Conan The Barbarian (1982)

You're such a tough guy, McManus. Do me a favor, right. Get the fuck off my dick. - Redfoot the Fence in The Usual Suspects (1995)

Fuck your father in the shower and then have a snack? Are you going to charge me dickhead? – Hockney in The Usual Suspects (1995)

You want to cut my throat, go ahead. You want to cut my fucking head off and use it for a fucking basketball? You can bowl with the motherfucker for all I care! Just don't let him do it! I don't want to get killed by this limey, immigrant jerkoff! I want get killed by an American jerkoff! - Gabriel Cash in Tango & Cash (1989)

Say what again. Say what again I dare you. I double dare you motherfucker. Say what again one more God dammed time. - Jules Winnfield in Pulp Fiction (1994)

You can beat us, chain us, lock us up. But we're gonna be back, understand? And when we do, cop, you better keep your ass off our turf, or we'll blow it off! Ya dig? We're Jezebels cop, remember that name. We'll be back! – Maggie in Switchblade Sisters (1975)

You punch like you take it up the ass! - Jake LaMotta in Raging Bull (1980)

I believe in death. I believe in disease. I believe in injustice and inhumanity, torture and anger and hate. I believe in murder. I believe in pain. I believe in cruelty and infidelity. I believe in slime and stink and every crawling, putrid thing Every possible ugliness and corruption, you son of a bitch. I believe...in you. - Detective Kinderman in The Exorcist III (1990)

I must break you. - Ivan Drago in in Rocky IV (1985)

Honey, you got real ugly. – Ash in Army of Darkness (1992)

When they send for you, you go in alive, you come out dead, and it's your best friend that does it. - Lefty in Donnie Brasco (1997)

Movie lines that leave you scratching your head and asking yourself if they meant for it to come off that way:

5. If Pazuzu comes for you, I will spit a leopard. - Kokumo in Exorcist II: The Heretic (1977)

4. Hey Leroy, I always did want to cornhole me a blind bitch! – Frank in Toxic Avenger (1984)

3. You're in big trouble though, pal. I eat pieces of shit like you for breakfast! – Shooter McGavin in Happy Gilmore (1996)

2. I used to fuck guys like you in Prison. - Jimmy in Road House (1989)

1. I only tell you one time. Don't fuck me Tony. Don't you ever try to fuck me. - Sosa in Scarface (1983)

Fredo, you're nothing to me now. You're not a brother, you're not a friend. I don't want to know you or what you do. I don't want to see you at the hotels, I don't want you near my house. When you see our mother, I want to know a day in advance, so I won't be there. You understand? - Michael Corleone in The Godfather Part II (1974)

Who's the black private dick that's a sex machine to all the chicks? – Shaft (1971) Can you dig it?

Don't let your mouth get your ass in trouble. - John Shaft in Shaft (1971)

Let's have a bachelor party with chicks and guns and fire trucks and hookers and drugs and booze! – Rudy in Bachelor Party (1984)

Well, suppose we ain't got no union cards and go in there and start playing anyway? Whatcha gonna do about that? You gonna stop us, Stein? Ha. You're gonna look pretty funny trying to eat corn on the cob with no fuckin' teeth! - Tucker McElroy in The Blues Brothers (1980)

What we were after now was the old surprise visit. That was a real kick and good for laughs and lashings of the old ultraviolent. – Alex in A Clockwork Orange (1971)

Well, if it isn't fat stinking billy goat Billy Boy in poison! How art thou, thou globby bottle of cheap, stinking chip-oil? Come and get one in the yarbles, if you have any yarbles, you eunuch jelly thou! – Alex in A Clockwork Orange (1971)

You won't get shit out of me. I've been constipated all week! - Hollis P. Wood in 1941 (1979)

Take your stinking paws off me, you damned dirty ape! – Taylor in Planet of The Apes (1968)

Very good. But brick not hit back! – Chong Li in Bloodsport (1998)

You break my record, now I break you, like I break your friend. – Chong Li in Bloodsport (1988)

You put a greased naked woman on all fours with a dog collar around her neck, and a leash, and a man's arm extended out up to here, holding onto the leash, and pushing a black glove in her face to sniff it. You don't find that offensive? You don't find that sexist? - Bobbi Flekman in This Is Spinal Tap (1984)

Fuck you. Gimme a bottle of booze, here's my dollar, suck my dick! – Fred in Street Trash (1987)

You made me break my hand completely off this time Tina! But I don't care darling, because I love you, and you've got to let me eat your brains! – Freddy in The Return of the Living Dead (1985)

If you're gonna ask if you can suck my left nut, the answer's maybe. - Artie DeVanzo in Beer League (2006)

Come on let's get this guy! Let's get this punk! He's nothin'! He's a loser! He's an asshole! A cock sucker! He's a total piece a shit! - Artie DeVanzo in Beer League (2006)

You motor boating son of a bitch! You old sailor you! Where is she? She still in the house? – Jeremy in Wedding Crashers (2005)

Your mom's a ukulele. – Terry in Reno 911!: Miami (2007)

Shut up, cunt. You louse. You got some fuckin' neck ain't you. Retired? Fuck off, you're revolting. Look at your sun tan, it's leather; it's like leather man, your skin. We could make a fucking suitcase out of you. Like a crocodile...fat crocodile. Fat bastard. You look like fucking Idi Amin, you know what I mean? Stay here? You should be ashamed of yourself. Who do you think you are? King of the castle? Cock of the walk? – Don in Sexy Beast (2000)

How do you like your ribs? - Jericho Action Jackson in Action Jackson (1988)

The man's son is a sexual psychopath! If I had family problems like that, I'd have myself neutered. – Jericho Action Jackson in Action Jackson (1988)

You are literally too stupid to insult. – Stu in The Hangover (2009)

If I wanted a joke, I'd follow you into the John and watch you take a leak. - Neal Page in Planes, Trains & Automobiles (1987)

Dumb sumbitch... - Buford T. Justice in Smokey and the Bandit (1977)

Nobody, and I mean nobody makes Sheriff Buford T. Justice look like a possum's pecker! - Buford T. Justice in Smokey and the Bandit (1977)

The last guy that made fun of my hair is still trying to pull his head outta his ass. – Yazz in Double Team (1997)

I'm an Earth sign. She's a Water sign. Together, we made mud. - Thornton Melon in Back to School (1986)

Brother man, this situation is rapidly becoming insalubrious...Meaning: We're about to stomp a mudhole in your ass! - Lt. Jackson in Dr. Black, Mr. Hyde (1976)

I smell skanks. Why don't you girls just pack it up before I leave tread marks on your face? – Letty in The Fast and the Furious (2001)

What Evelle here is trying to say is that we felt that the institution no longer had anything to offer us. – Gale Snoats in Raising Arizona (1987)

You want to find an outlaw, hire an outlaw. You want to find a Dunkin' Donuts, call a cop. - Leonard Smalls in Raising Arizona (1987)

This country is going to the dogs. You know, it used to be when you bought a politician, that son of a bitch stayed bought. – Roy Fuchs in Used Cars (1980)

A wise man's life is based around fuck you. The United States of America is based on fuck you. You have a navy? Greatest army in the history of mankind? Fuck you! Blow me. We'll fuck it up ourselves. – Frank in The Gambler (2014)

They are so poor... that they only have one God! But we Romans are rich. We've got a lot of gods. We've got a god for everything. The only thing we don't have a god for is premature ejaculation... but I hear that's coming quickly. – Comicus in History of the World: Part I (1981)

I fucked her brains out... for eleven seconds! - Jordan Belfort in The Wolf of Wall Street (2013)

Let me tell you something. There's no nobility in poverty. I've been a poor man, and I've been a rich man. And I choose rich every fucking time. - Jordan Belfort in The Wolf of Wall Street (2013)

I am a musician and the monkey is a businessman. He doesn't tell me what to play, and I don't tell him what to do with his money. – Beggar in The Return of the Pink Panther (1975)

Hey, Dr. Jones, no time for love. We've got company. – Short Round in Indiana Jones and the Temple of Doom (1984)

Mola Ram! Prepare to meet Kali... in Hell! - Indiana Jones in Indiana Jones and the Temple of Doom (1984)

Show's over, motherfuckers. – Hit Girl in Kick-Ass (2010)

What are you, some fucking asshole? Or are you just taking lessons? - Borelli's Man in State of Grace (1990)

Listen up, maggots. You are not special. You are not a beautiful or unique snowflake. You're the same decaying organic matter as everything else. - Tyler Durden in Fight Club (1999)

I'd suck a fart out her asshole and hold it like a bong hit. – Stu in Good Luck Chuck (2007)

Cause she's got a great ass... and you got your head all the way up it! - Vincent Hanna in Heat (1995)

I'm angry. I'm very angry, Ralph. You know, you can ball my wife if she wants you to. You can lounge around here on her sofa, in her ex-husband's dead-tech, post-modernistic bullshit house if you want to. But you do not get to watch my fucking television set! - Vincent Hanna in Heat (1995)

If it looks like shit, and it sounds like shit, than it must be shit. - Jack Horner in Boogie Nights (1997)

All work and no play makes Jack a dull boy. - Jack Torrance in The Shining (1980)

Wendy? Darling? Light, of my life. I'm not gonna hurt you. You didn't let me finish my sentence. I said, I'm not gonna hurt you. I'm just going to bash your brains in. Gonna bash 'em right the fuck in! - Jack Torrance in The Shining (1980)

You're not a neighbor. You're a drug dealer whose apartment smells like cheese and feet. - Rose O'Reilly in We're the Millers (2013)

My longest relationship was, like, six months, and then she farted in her sleep. I'm like: I'm out of here, man, and I was gone before she woke up. – Guy in Ted (2012)

I say, why don't you guys locate your dicks, remove the shrink wrap, and fucking use them! - Steve Stifler in American Pie (1999)

He puts his dick in your mouth while you were asleep! – Pete in Neighbors (2014)

I hope that when the world comes to an end, I can breathe a sigh of relief, because there will be so much to look forward to. – Donnie in Donnie Darko (2001)

I can feel the juices rushing back to my balls as we speak. - Paul Vitti in Analyze This (1999)

If you ever disrespect my wife again, I will end you. I will fucking end you. You got that, chief? – Sean in Good Will Hunting (1997)

Fuck you, fuck you, fuck you, you're cool, and fuck you, I'm out! – Scarface in Half Baked (1998)

Also Available from the Author

Documenting Danny Marianino's days as a metalhead from childhood into adulthood, Don't Ever Punch a Rockstar somehow rationalizes playing in a few hardcore/punk bands, touring, fighting, drinking, internet bullying, celebrity encounters, satanic curses, house fires, harassment and collecting an immeasurable amount of hate mail from some of the most illiterate human beings the world has to offer.

Though Oprah will never add this into her book club, it's still a good lesson in accepting the negative with a laugh and gaining a new sense of temperance and humility. At the very least it will entertain you with a campy memoir and a detailed eye-opening account of the chaos that followed the infamous event that VH1 called one of the Most Shocking Moments in Rock and Roll.

This is by no means the same old autobiography that you have read before. Don't Ever Punch a Rockstar combine elements of Get in The Van, Emails from and Asshole and Shit My Dad Says all in one hot mess of a story.

"Danny Marianino's Don't Ever Punch A Rockstar is a sock in the jaw to punk/metal scene conformity, and it hurts so good!" - STEVEN BLUSH, author/filmmaker, American Hardcore

Available on Amazon Paperback and Kindle, Nook and through SmashWords. Com

You can also order through Barnes and Noble and Interpunk .Com

For wholesale and distro inquires for my books please contact Createspace. Com

Also Available from the Author

For most of us, revenge is a dish best served....right now. Whether you're a die-hard fan of revenge films or just someone who enjoys seeing a good dose of vindication, this remarkably diverse genre gives notoriety to

heroes, villains, and most importantly, the underdogs, who use humor, suspense, and sometimes, sheer mind blowing terror to inflict payback on someone (or thing) who had it coming.

In The Mega Book of Revenge Films Vol. 1: The Big Payback, author Danny Marianino takes you on a ruthless journey with the most comprehensive film guide that includes the best and worst of cinema's retaliation flicks. Be prepared for Avenging Nuns, Armed Vagrants,

Urban Anti-Heroes, Lone Wolves, Kung-Fu Masters and Demons from The Beyond that are just a sample of some of the hundreds of movies referenced inside.

This book is an essential guide for the revenge film fan of all ages as Marianino presents a unique and exciting look into the genre while he explores some of the greatest moments from the big and small screen. You will love remembering the quotes and taglines that made you laugh, cheer, and wince as you revisit these amazing films through interviews, articles, and Marianino's tremendous sense of humor.

"Every so often, a revenge film can take us to places where we question humankind's everlasting lust for violence, it's cost and effect. But mostly it's about visceral enjoyment of seeing the odds evened and the balance restored...Clearly Marianino has done his homework." – Tal Zimerman, writer, Rue Morgue Magazine

Available on Amazon. Wholesale inquires for books please contact Createspace. Com

ABOUT THE AUTHOR

Danny Marianino is a New Jersey native that now lives in Scottsdale Arizona with his wife and three mental dogs. He authored his first book Don't Ever Punch a Rockstar: A Collection of Hate Mail and Other Crazy Rumors in 2012 and has since released a few other genre books.

He is a horror programmer for the Phoenix Film Festival and The International Horror and Sci-Fi Festival and also owned the website I Can Smell Your Brains. Com with his good buddy Brandon Kinchen.

While it's painfully obvious he has an affinity for all things cinema, Danny has a huge bobble head collection and is also addicted to buying old MAD Magazines. He spends his evenings glued to The El Rey Network and spends hours changing the order on his Netflix Queue. He is an avid collector of horror magazines as well and has a 'dude room' dedicated to an overwhelming amount of nonsense. Danny has also played guitar in a few bands and has released a bunch of albums worldwide.

Honestly, he is a pretty cool guy. I'm not just saying that because I am writing about myself either.

For news on my future books and other interesting things be sure to visit: **dannymarianino.com**

.

Printed in Great Britain
by Amazon